▲ Mimi cave art, western Arnhem Land (Baldwin Spencer collection).

▲ Stone tjuringa from MacDonnell Ranges, NT.

The art of Australia's Aboriginals reflects their traditional way of life: monumental sculpture is not for nomads and those who seek no shelter but that provided by caves and bark rainbreaks have no mind for fragile treasures nor the temples and palaces needed to store them. The artist is restricted to the materials of his physical surroundings and the natural environment must provide both the medium and the means of protection for his fixed permanent art. So the Australian Aboriginal painted on sheltered cave walls, carved on living trees, engraved on flat exposed outcrops of rock; his portable art was confined to sacred objects such as *tjuringa*—small decorated stones which embodied the totemic ancestors—and to things which he had to carry around anyway—boomerangs, spears, dillybags, and such like.

Much of his art was temporary, created for a particular purpose and intended to last only a short time. In the red earth of the Centre, ground paintings of intricate design were wrought with painstaking ritual, hardened with human blood—and then the labour of hours was obliterated when the ritual was over. The legends of creation were painted on bark by the elders of Arnhem Land, who told the tale to the young initiates ... and discarded the scripts. Elaborate body decorations for sacred corroborees took many days to prepare, though their role in the actual play might be measured in minutes. Carved shapes, some by tradition gouged out only by human fingernails, were chopped up after the ceremony, burnt, or thrown into a sacred waterhole. A man might trace a story in sand to beguile his child, then watch it wiped clean by wind and tide. Or paint his hopes and triumphs on the bark sheets which sheltered him during the wet season and would be discarded in the Dry.

Art was an essential ingredient of Aboriginal life, permeating every aspect, both ceremonial and secular. It was sorcery and magic, and the expression of deeply held religious beliefs, the source of fertility and natural increase, the saga of achievements and the daily record of gossip, hunting, loves and hates. Form and style varied from place to place, influenced and limited by the tools and materials available, but recurrent throughout the continent was the theme of the creation myths, the Australian genesis, which stimulated art in all its forms. Almost without exception Aboriginals tell of a time beyond memory when the earth was flat and featureless and there were no flowers, no food, no people. Then sometime, somehow, out of the earth or out of the sea, travelling over the edge of the world or descending from the skies, came the creative heroes. They walked upon the land and decreed what should exist. Gullies appeared where they dug the earth, and streams where they urinated. They were usually flexible in form, sometimes human, sometimes animal, sometimes male and sometimes female, and they created everything. They gave birth to man and the other creatures; they converted one another into trees and rock formations. Maybe they threw one of their number into the sky to make the moon or cast a woman up to gather the yams that shine there as stars. Everything that moved on earth, everything that grew and everything that had substance or form was created by these various beings, who defined codes of conduct for animals and men and created the rituals which the tribes must follow. Then they left, sometimes turning themselves into sacred objects, sometimes sinking into a rock face, leaving an impression for men to see and trace with paint.

Spirit figures such as these occur in caves throughout the

◀ Quinkans supervise initiations in cave near Laura, Qld.

▲ Spirit figures at Sickness Dreaming Place, Sleisbeck, Arnhem Land.

continent, particularly in the north-west. A well-known example is the Wandjina paintings of the Central Kimberleys which aroused considerable interest when first described early last century, mainly because of their white bodies and halo-like headdresses which led to some fanciful theories linking them with Christian myths. Aboriginals definitely do not consider these paintings to be the original work of any human artist (though men have the responsibility to freshen up the colours from time to time), but believe them to be the actual creative heroes, the Wandjina themselves. The spirit figures shown here are at the Sickness Dreaming Place (Healing Site) at Sleisbeck, near El Shirana, Arnhem Land. They are typical of the tradition: large, white-bodied, outlined in red. This combination of red and white, common in such figures, reflects the fertility colours of water and blood.

Another recurring theme in Aboriginal art is that of the stick-like magic-makers, of which the Mimis of western Arnhem

◀ Rock engravings, Ku-ring-gai, near Sydney, NSW.

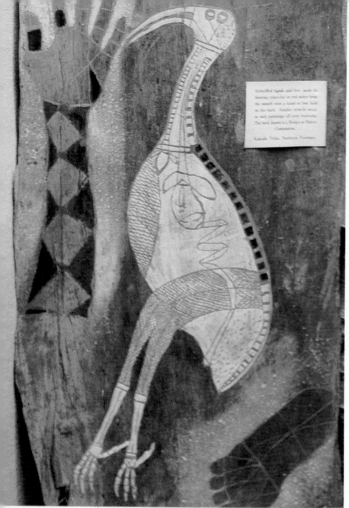

▲ Bark painting from Oenpelli district, western Arnhem Land.

▲ 'Thin man' paintings, Noarlangie Rocks, NT.

Land are an example. The Aboriginals say that these strangely graceful paintings depicting people in action—running, leaping, fighting, dancing—are the self-portraits of fairy-like creatures who live in rock crevices and come out only at night. They are so delicate that they can hunt only in still weather, lest their bones be broken by the wind. Their sight and hearing are so keen that no one can creep up on them unawares; they flee into their rock havens and blow on the cave wall, causing it to open like a door and close after them. So it is that Aboriginals never see them, though they say they can hear them scampering around the rocks at night. 'Mimi' is a name which comes from western Arnhem Land and is confined to that area, but the stick-man style of painting is widespread in Australia and there are similar figures, almost always doing the same sort of things and linked with similar legends though known by other names and sometimes nameless. Such paintings are apparently relics of an older era

◄ Wessell Island cave painting tells story of the 'monkey ship'.

6

▲ Footprints of Baiame on sandstone near Sydney.

▲ Pecked intaglios, Mootwingie, NSW.

of cave art and the myths surrounding them a means of explaining the work of forgotten artists. The long-bodied 'thin men' of Noarlangie Rocks are representative of a somewhat similar art form about which very little is known. This style extends across the north of Australia into the Quinkan country of Queensland. Unlike the Mimis, thin men are usually inactive. They are sometimes shown with arms and legs flexed upwards at an angle, praying-mantis fashion, and may feature headdresses of a style not now seen anywhere in Australia.

In western Arnhem Land these older forms are often overlaid with the striking x-ray art of the district, a technique apparently developed at a later date and still practised by present-day Aboriginals. X-ray paintings are essentially static, and show not only the external form but also what is known to be there yet cannot be seen—the skeleton of an animal, the heart, lungs and other organs. These paintings cover the walls and ceilings of rock shelters in great profusion. They are made on bark as well as rock, and are used for hunting and fishing magic and also for teaching: for example, to show the internal structure of an animal or how the meat should be divided in accordance with custom.

Some Aboriginal art was purely secular, recording events of the day, so that caves became the archives of the community. Thus Djingalou, pictured here drawing in his cave gallery at Wessel Island, depicts the monkey of the *Sea Fox*; this vessel was stranded on the beach of Elcho Island in 1959 and had on board actor-magician John Calvert and also a chimpanzee, animal star of the Tarzan series. The incident had a tremendous impact on the local Aboriginals who had never before seen a monkey and were astounded by a man who could make things disappear before their eyes.

Wish-fulfilment art, associated with magic and sorcery, is found throughout Australia. With the aid of *puri-puri*, pain-

Rock engraving, Bantry Bay, near Sydney. ▶

▲ Baiame and Daramulen, creative heroes of the sandstone tribes.

▲ Unusually large pecked intaglio, Mootwingie, NSW.

▲ Rubbed grooves near bank of Macquarie River, NSW.

ted on bark or perhaps the wall of a well-hidden cave, a man may sing a woman to bed or an enemy to his downfall. These dream-come-true paintings are touched-up with ritual and the chanting of charms. Some, particularly those associated with wounding and death, are crude, as they may have to be done with great secrecy and of necessity speed, perhaps slapped on by a man in a rage who has dashed off from the group, crawled under an overhanging rock, and must create his puri-puri before his absence is noticed; others are major works, carefully executed. The rock paintings of northern Queensland which show white men falling from horses or coming to grief in some other fashion are believed to be puri-puris, and the huge petroglyphs of the Hawkesbury sandstone country of New South Wales, depicting great schools of fish or a man in the act of spearing a kangaroo, are probably wish-fulfilment art associated with hunting magic.

Rock engravings or petroglyphs are the most enduring form of Aboriginal art, occurring on suitable rock formations throughout the mainland and Tasmania. Many are of great antiquity, some are less than a century old, but most must be classed as prehistoric simply because early European settlers did not seek to learn or record their significance before the culture which created them became extinct. The earliest type of rock art probably consisted of rubbed grooves and might well have originated from the shaping and sharpening of implements on a suitable stone surface, forming by chance patterns and simple designs of parallel, crossed and radiating lines. Pounded designs formed by banging on the surface of the rock with a hard pebble until the outer patina was broken and the colour of the inner rock revealed were also a feature of ancient rock art, though both techniques continued in use side by side with later developments right up until the coming of the white man. Very old examples cover only a small range of motifs based on concentric circles, lines, and rows of rounded holes.

Early pecked petroglphys featured similar designs. Pictured (page 10) is one near Broken Hill, New South Wales, with concentric circles and line patterns which may represent bird and animal tracks and possibly stylised men. Present-day Aboriginals deny all knowledge of these carvings, saying they were made by the people of the Dreamtime, though similar

◀ Pounded rock designs, Ord River, WA.

▲ Huge petroglyph at Ku-ring-gai; the whale is 20 metres long.

▲ Rock engravings, Ku-ring-gai, probably hunting magic.

▲ Stone arrangement, Gibraltar National Park, NSW.

▲ Early pecked petroglyphs, Broken Hill, NSW.

symbols survive in the ritual art of central Australia. The only known examples of the art of the Tasmanians are also in this category.

Pecked petroglyphs were made by striking the rock surface with a pointed stone or shell so as to form a series of punctures which usually overlapped into a continuous groove but were sometimes left as a line of separated pits. This technique widened the range of Aboriginal rock art; development of outline engraving enabled the naturalistic portrayal of animals, men and culture heroes and these took their place beside the geometric motifs of an earlier era. The outline style of rock engraving reached its zenith in the Sydney-Hawkesbury district of New South Wales, doubtless due to the great areas of suitable stone available there. More than four thousand figures have been recorded, some of immense size. These outline engravings are usually in groups, in places comprising a hundred or more figures and covering a hectare of flat, exposed sandstone. They include a wide range of subjects—men, women and mythical beings,

◀ Emu, Ku-ring-gai Chase National Park.

whales, fish, marsupials, birds and reptiles, animal and other tracks, weapons and implements. Most are life-size or larger, some are gigantic; the whale shown on page 9, apparently in the act of swallowing a man, is 20 metres long, and the creative heroes, Baiame the Sky-father and his brother/son Daramulen (page 8), are portrayed as 18 or so metres tall. These galleries of the Hawkesbury sandstone country appear to be associated with either hunting and fishing magic, religious rituals such as initiation, or both—animal figures were no doubt used to depict tribal totems as well as to promote or record successful hunting. Groups of engravings sometimes appear to be linked, with human or animal tracks pointing the way from one series to the other, and most likely these formed a sequence, each section of which portrayed portion of the myths of creation and the travels of the culture heroes. Sometimes the footprint tracks are huge (see page 7) and since the Aboriginal rarely exagererated the size of a track (his living depended upon instant and accurate recognition) it must be that these are the marks of Baiame himself.

A later development from the basic style of punctured outline was the pecked intaglio, in which the whole surface of the engraving was hollowed out in reverse relief. Many thousands have been found in western New South Wales and eastern South Australia engraved on the rocks around waterholes. Most of these intaglios are small, though larger figures are sometimes featured, such as the kangaroo pictured on page 8.

Other forms of Aboriginal fixed art were the symbolic stone arrangements at bora grounds and increase sites throughout the continent, and the carved trees or dendroglyphs of eastern Australia, which were limited to New South Wales and some parts of southern Queensland. Dendroglyphs are the only example of massive carving in Aboriginal art. Symbolic designs, usually geometric, were carved on the living tree with axes and touched up from time to time to prevent the bark growing over the pattern and obliterating it. They

Carved tree (dendroglyph), Parkes district, NSW. ▶

▼ Deeper systematised petroglyph, Mount Cameron West, Tas.

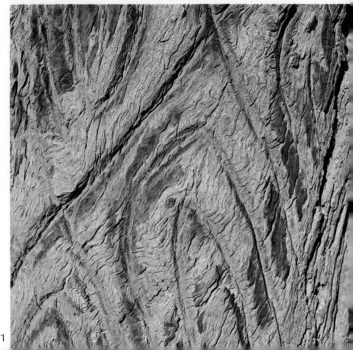

Carving on burial tree, Dubbo, NSW. ▶

▲ Snake creative being, Nama Cave, Yuendumu.

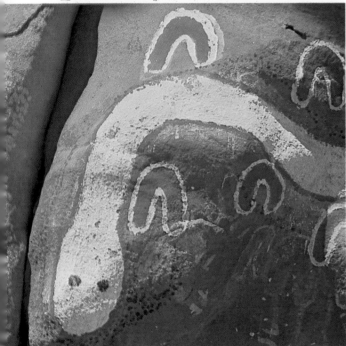

were associated with initiation ceremonies and burial rites. (The only other example of decorated trees occurs in the Kimberleys, north-western Australia, where naturalistic designs are scratched rather than carved in the soft bark of the baobabs.)

Cave paintings are the most common form of Aboriginal fixed art, for this medium gave the artist considerably more scope than did the laborious techniques of rock engraving. Pigments used are those of the earth—natural ochres of red and yellow, white pipeclay, black manganese oxide or, if this is not available, crushed charcoal and charred bark. Most pigments were obtained locally or by barter, though in some cases Aboriginals journeyed hundreds of miles to collect ochre from a particular locality because of special mythological associations. Dr Basedow tells of the Yarrakinna red ochre deposit in the Flinders Ranges, South Australia, regarded as the blood of a sacred emu and visited by Aboriginals as far distant as the 'Salt-water Tribe' of Queensland. Other sacred ochre mines are at Wilgamia in Western Australia (red and yellow, the blood and liver of a mythical kangaroo) and at Tempe Downs in the Northern Territory. Judging from the extensive excavations, some of these workings have been in use for many centuries.

The artist's palette is a flat stone on which the hard pigments are ground to a powder, then mixed with water or natural fixatives such as emu fat, eggs of the sea-going turtle, wax and

◀ The direction of the snake's head was changed recently.

honey of the wild bee and sap from tree orchids. Brushes are made from chewed twigs, narrow strips of stringybark, palm leaves and feathers. In large paintings the forefinger and even the palm of the hand is used to apply the paint, and pigments are sometimes blown from the mouth; stencils, the most widely distributed technique of all, are made by spraying liquid pigment from the mouth onto an object held against the surface of the rock (or occasionally by blowing dry ochre onto a dampened surface.) Stencils of the hand are the most common, the simplest, and possibly the earliest form of cave art, and occur as the only motif in some rock shelters. Favoured colours for such stencils are white or red, and in the Oenpelli district of western Arnhem Land the hand and arm are sometimes coloured inside as well and decorated with elaborate line designs. Cave paintings occur throughout the continent, but the richest and most spectacular galleries are in the north, and here, in some cases, it is still possible to find out the traditional meaning of much of the sacred art. The huge snake depicted in the Nama Cave near Yuendumu in Arnhem Land (pictured opposite) is a typical creative being, who according to legend travelled through the area, carried on the shoulders of a number of man-like beings. Some time ago there was a theological argument between various groups of those responsible for the maintenance of the cave, about the way this totemic creator should face. Every detail of his travels was known, for the records had been handed down to the present members of the group by word of mouth for generations. They knew, for example, that when the snake and his escorts passed this cave and his image was recorded there in paint, he was travelling at right angles to the face of the rock shelter; the argument between the two groups was concerned about

Combination hand stencil and x-ray painting, Oenpelli, NT. ▶

▼ Aboriginal cave art, Musgrave Ranges, SA.

▲ Cave painting of turtle near Cooktown, Qld.

13

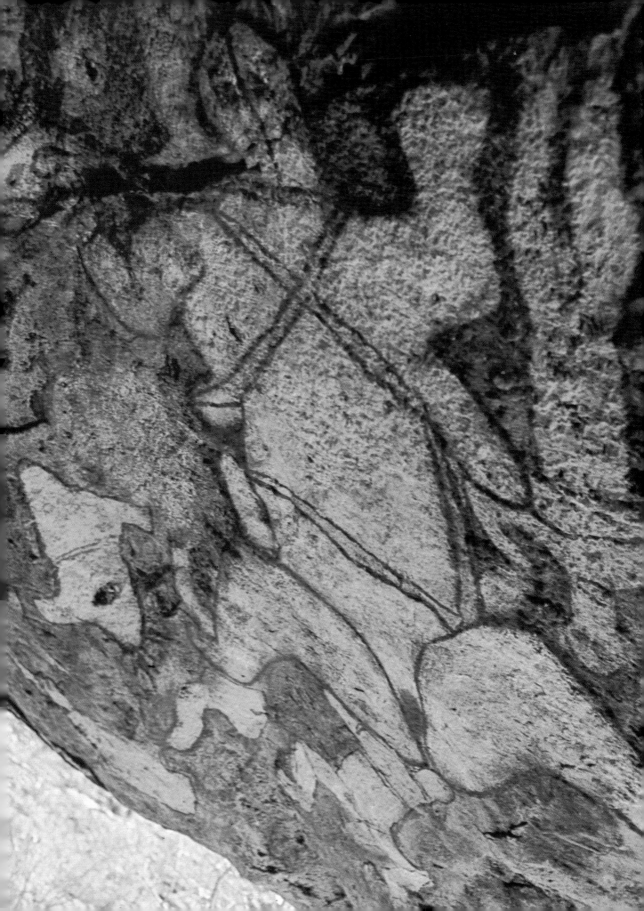

which way the head should face. Not only this: they argued also about whether the creative being should be depicted as having a red body outlined in white, or whether his body should be white and the outline red. Eventually the 'reform group' won the argument, and though the snake has been recorded by some anthropologists (and photographed by Mountford) as being red with a white outline, and facing one way, it has now been turned around and the body is white, outlined in red.

The U-shaped figures above and below the snake represent the shoulders of the men who carried it on its travels. Today, when increase rites are performed, men paint themselves in such a way that, when viewed from the side, this same U-shape can be seen on their shoulders, supporting the 'snake' which is represented by the headdresses they wear. The men crawl along on their knees, and as they do so the snake wriggles along a part of the trail it followed in the Dreamtime. To the left of the snake are vertical strokes in white. These are the spears of the men who carried the snake, painted where they left them leaning against the wall of the cave when they rested there on their travels. The Nama snake paintings are so sacred that only twice-initiated men, approaching middle age, can view them.

In the wild and weird country of Cape York Peninsula dwell Quinkans, terrifying figures of Aboriginal mythology that lurk beyond the light of the campfire waiting a chance to steal the kidney fat from the belly of the unwary and fill the cavity with green tree ants. Quinkans reflect tribal marriage customs and restrictions; they are distorted and malformed because they broke those laws. They live in crevices in caves and their images are marked on the walls. In a cave in the hills above Laura towers Big Uncle Quinkan. He fixes his eye on all new initiates who enter his cave, warning them of their duties—to men and to 'man's things' and to all the people of the tribe.

In an area of Arnhem Land from Sleisbeck to El Shirana, the creative being Nargorkun and his wives, the Narlinji-linji, lived and left their records on the walls of caves. This area, about five hundred square kilometres, is known as 'Sickness Country'. The location is impressive—high on the central plateau of Arnhem Land with access from all sides through deep gorges in the steep rocky escarpment. Of the three main sites recorded (by William Arndt) the most important is the Sickness Dreaming Place at Sleisbeck (pictured opposite and on page 5). Consisting of waterhole, road and cave, it was used for sickness and healing rites, the seclusion and training of adolescent, and was also the mythical home of the creator of all the earth and its people.

The myths of Nargorkun the creator say he was a short, thick-set man, who wore a feather headdress and carried a stone axe with which he made the lightning. One day he was bitten by Palmura the mud-dauber hornet, which caused him to swell up into all manner of monstrous shapes. He became very sick and thirsty and so badly crippled that he had to crawl on hands and knees to move about. After drinking at the Sickness Waterhole he crawled up and over the ridge to the Sickness Cave or Home for Sick People. Behind him he left a well-defined path, the Sickness Road, and his story and shades on the walls of the Sickness Cave. Then he entered the ground to rest. There he will remain, harmless and peaceful, unless disturbed by undue noise, when he will wake up, and, by lifting himself, split open the world and destroy it. There is a damp rock in the cave which must not be allowed to dry

▲ Quinkan of Split Rock, Qld.; he makes the thunder.

Stick-like Quinkan figure, Laura, north Qld. ▶

15

out, for if it does it will catch fire and cover the whole countryside with ashes. Nargorkun had two wives, sisters who seem to typify the ideal Aboriginal woman. They now live with him under the floor of the cave. As Nargorkun was too sick to hunt for himself, he had two young boys to do this for him, and the shades of the various animals caught by these two were left on the walls. This was to remind the young of their responsibilities to the aged, the sick and the infirm. Also portrayed are the punishments he inflicted on youths who failed to obey his law: offenders were reduced to skeletons, to ghosts, to handprints on the cave walls. Ceremonies at the sickness place were held yearly. The men gathered at the waterhole, chanted sickness songs and danced their dances, then crawled up the sickness road, as Nargorkun had done, on hands and knees. Each carried with him a bone, either of a deceased friend or of an animal they usually hunted. They moved with extreme care, noiselessly and only into the wind; stones were not bumped and even blades of grass were moved gently aside with a woomera. The bones were deposited on a large heap on the floor of the cave and the men chanted their homage songs, but only softly because Nargorkun was sleeping beneath the ground. The photograph on page 5 shows Nargorkun wearing his headdress and carrying the axe with which he made the lightning. His initiation marks are clearly visible, as is the mark of his circumcision. One of the Narlinji-linji is on his left, and he is shown again (right) with both women beside him. The childbirth painting (page 14) is regarded by Arndt as a clue to the hidden meaning of the sickness myths. Nargorkun is described as the creator of all things, yet his wives are shown in childbirth and we are told they helped him in the process of creation. This inconsistency and the juxtaposition of childbirth scenes and the distorted Nargorkun lend weight to Arndt's theory which suggests that the sickness cult is an expression of man's subconscious feelings of inadequacy in the face of women's role in childbirth; that Nargorkun's bodily distortions mimicked those of pregnancy and his 'sickness' was sympathetic labour; but that since he had no vulva the child he created by these distortions was transferred to the women to be born. The huge monolith of central Australia, which the Aboriginals call Uluru and the white man Ayers Rock, is the

▲ The shallow caves are crowded with Aboriginal art.

▼ Ayers Rock and the Olgas, central Australia.

▲ Figures in cave, Ayers Rock; dark streaks are long-dried blood.

▼ Fig-tree man wearing nuiti (rayed headdress).

▼ Paintings of sacred objects: kulpidji (top) and nurtunja (below).

Dreaming Place of the Pitjantjatjara people and plays an important role in their lives. Its shallow caves are crowded with paintings portraying the totemic beings who made it and the legends of their creative activities. Uluru, the legends say, was formed during the *tjukurapa* (Dreamtime) and many myths explain the making of the various features of that great red rock. Charles Mountford describes the paintings and legends of Uluru in his book, *Ayers Rock,—Its People, Their Beliefs and Their Art*. He visited the Rock several times over a period of twenty years (1940-60) and witnessed the actual production of some of the paintings, recording their meaning from the artists themselves. Many of the designs are abstract, making interpretation virtually impossible without such first-hand explanation.

Body decorations, Elcho Island, NT. ▶

▼ Man in mourning mud, Elcho Island.

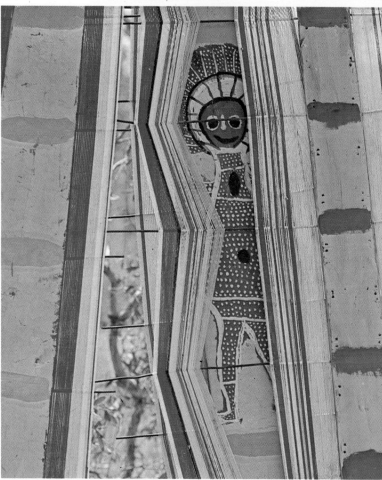

▲ Ceremonial headdress, Derby, WA.

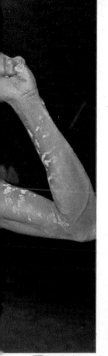

▼ Feathered ceremonial pole, Elcho Island, NT.

▼ Corroboree headdress, Derby, WA.

▼ Sacred corroboree, Derby; dancers decorate bodies with birds' down and balance huge headdresses on shoulders.

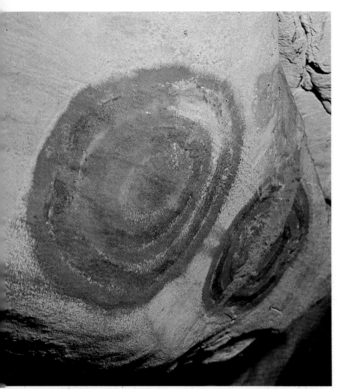

▲ Cave painting, Reedy Rockhole, near Kings Canyon, NT.

On the north-west wall of Uluru is a 27-metre long cave used for initiation ceremonies. Day-to-day secular art as well as paintings of sacred significance occur there, but since women were forbidden to enter and the cave was never used as a camping ground, its walls are not as crowded as those of most of Uluru's rock shelters. The men of the Mala (hare-wallaby) totem tell how this cave was made in the Dreamtime from the hard base of a termite mound turned to stone by the blood shed following rituals of circumcision and sub-incision—for after they had completed initiation of the young men, the adult Mala men opened veins in their own arms and let their blood fall to the ground. The male and female figures shown on page 16 and the back cover are in this cave, and the dark stains below them are the blood of Mala men; traditionally men of this totem, when they visit Uluru, open veins in their arms and allow their blood to flow down the back wall of the initiation cave, which is marked for most of its length with dark streaks of long-dried blood. No information is available about these particular figures, which portray the women with initiation scars and exaggerated genitals, but Mountford himself witnessed the painting of the figure with rayed headdress in the same cave (pictured lower left, page 17) and recorded details of the myth it illustrates. It was painted by Moanya in 1940 and symbolises the fig-tree man of Jirin-jirin. His head is represented by a circle, surrounded by a rayed headdress which, the artist told Mountford, was the *nuiti* worn by the fig-tree man of creation times and by those who, in present-day rituals, act out his role to ensure a plentiful supply of figs. Clad in this traditional headdress and with body bearing the correct markings, each man becomes himself the creative being and possesses his power; they dance around the sacred fig-trees of Jirin-jirin, 'water' them with blood from their arm-veins, and thus ensure the fertility of fig-trees everywhere in the world.

On the western face of Uluru, a little south of the initiation cave, are two groups of paintings, one above the other. The golden figure with rayed headdress shown on page 17 is one of several designs in the lower cave. The Aboriginals explained to Mountford that it was a representation of a ceremonial body decoration. The elliptical objects (lower right, page 17) are in the longer, upper cave. Mountford was told that these represented a *kulpidji* and a *nurtunja* pole. A nurtunja is a ceremonial pole of totemic significance, usually decorated with a tuft of feathers at the top. Size is variable and they may be carried in the hand, set in the ground or worn on the head (an example of this type of ceremonial object is shown on page 19). Kulpidji are the most sacred possessions of the Pitjantjatjara tribe. They are the repository of the very essence of life; women and uninitiated youths are not allowed to touch them, see them or even know of their existence. The one depicted in the cave at Uluru is decorated with bird's down, symbolised by radiating lines around the edge.
Featherdown, a feature of sacred patterns in central and northern areas, is also widely used in body decorations for totemic and initiation rituals; it is usually stuck on with blood, a most effective adhesive as well as the powerful and mystical substance of life. Ceremonial decorations, which include elaborate headdresses and hand-held objects, are sacred art indeed for they transform the participants into the totemic

◀ Witchetty grub totemic signs, Emily Gap, NT.

▲ Waninga of the Pariltja (snake) totem, central Australia.

▼ Sacred tjuringa, carved stone embodying totemic ancestor.

▼ Totemic symbols, Nama Cave, Yuendumu.

▲ Unusual coloured tjuringa from Halls's Creek, WA.

ancestors themselves, to once again act out the Dreamtime travels of the heroes and re-create the animals and plants for the use of the tribe today. Red and yellow ochres and white pipeclay are also used for body decorations, in patterns ranging from daubs and smears to complex designs so highly formalised that their meaning is known only to the initiates. Clay over the headdress and clay over the head make the headdress part of the man and the man part of the headdress; the whole may be decorated with twigs and grass and feather-plumes, bound on with string made from human hair. These headdresses and body decorations, together with ground paintings and sacred objects, might take days or weeks to prepare; the purpose of the ceremony is religious but as so much time is occupied with making the necessary works of art it is a moot point which is the most important. Corroboree art is a very fixed form, more so than any other; the ritual is as decreed by the heroes and cannot be changed without jeopardising the continuation of food supplies and life itself, a risk that the Aboriginals are not prepared to take. Ground drawings in the Northern Territory have not altered in the past century of observation despite vast changes in other spheres.

Art also plays its part in Aboriginal mortuary rites. In north-eastern Arnhem Land the skulls of the dead are decorated with the personal and clan totemic symbols and may be carried around for years as a mark of respect; a widow may wear her husband's skull as a pendant, or a relative may carry it about as the tribe moves from place to place. In many northern areas the bodies of mourners and mourned alike are decorated with elaborate and often fantastic designs. The carved and painted burial poles of the Tiwi people (Bathurst and Melville Islanders) are among the most spectacular art objects of the Australian Aboriginals. Made from a single tree trunk up to six metres high, they are decorated with traditional designs representing the totem of the deceased

◄ Decorated skull, north-eastern Arnhem Land.

▼ Utilitarian and totemic objects alike are decorated.

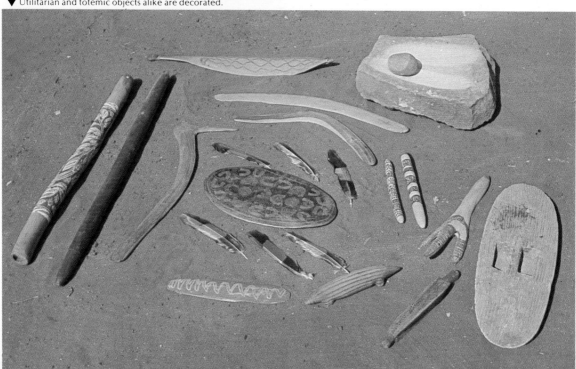

▲ Totemic art, Nama Cave, Yuendumu.

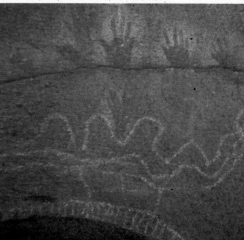

▲ Rock engraving of creative serpent, Yilgarnia, WA.

▲ Sacred totemic poles (rangga) on display at Elcho Island.
The strange smiling faces of Cleland Hills, central Australia. ▶

and often a stylised ship's mast, symbol of farewell which dates back to the Macassan traders of past centuries, who erected the masts of their vessels before unfurling sails and returning to their homeland. Sometimes a dozen or more such poles are made and erected during ceremonies lasting many months. Not all carved poles are associated with death; in north-east Arnhem Land and adjacent islands there are totemic poles of great significance and exceptional beauty. These are the *rangga*, sacred objects similar in purpose to tjuringa, except that there is only one for each totemic group, rather than one for each man. Tribal Aboriginals regard them very highly and are most secretive about them, often giving misleading information. Rangga are normally kept in a cave; they can only be brought out on special occasions, must never be viewed by women and seldom by the uninitiated. Dramatic ritual accompanies production from their secret hiding places; they are usually brought out on the backs of crawling men, balanced on their necks and produced with great ceremony. An exception of considerable interest to anthropologists is the public display of rangga on Elcho Island. R. M. Berndt (1958) describes this as an adjustment movement and records that it followed the inadvertent showing of a film featuring sacred rangga to an unrestricted audience at the mission church. In an unprecedented break with tradition the tribal elders decided to put the rangga on public display and link them with the power of the mission by the creation of additional rangga symbolising Christianity. By thus evaluating the old life in terms of what they regarded as the new, they hoped to maintain a balance between local tradition and the world that was impinging on it from the outside and so preserve the identity and culture of eastern Arnhem Landers while at the same time enabling them to retain whatever advantages the new life had to offer. Sadly the rangga of Elcho today look rather neglected; colours of some have faded and others have been attacked by termites. Pictured (opposite) is the section facing the beach; it was photographed in 1969. According to Berndt the rangga on the left is a *djanda* (goanna) on *djuda* (tree) rangga, one of the most important of those associated with the Djanggawul myths; the round rangga is the djuda with the goanna carved on it in relief and the painted lines represent sandhills with small plants. Alongside is another djuda rangga with goanna, this time squared; down two sides is a design representing spring water running and the other sides feature goanna.

Sacred totemic art is non-figurative—the art of 'circle, line and square', as anthropologist T. G. H. Strehlow describes it. Concentric designs are numerous; they are a feature of the totemic symbols of the Nama Snake cave at Yuendumu (page 21), the ground paintings and other ritual art of central Australia, and also the art of the lost Tasmanians (page 11). It could be that the art of central Australia has remained static in form for the ten thousand years or so that Tasmania was cut off from the mainland, for the two areas have in common a degree of isolation and a cultural similarity in the existence of these totemic designs and the lack of figurative art. Apart from a few crude human shapes in both areas, there are few known attempts by native artists to portray animals and plants as they are; commonly, these are represented by their orifices. Startling examples of this art style are the smiling faces of the Cleland Hills, central Australia, formed from circles and semi-circles, five thousand years or more ago; but these are not entirely inconsistent, for they are figurative representations of humans achieved in the manner of non-

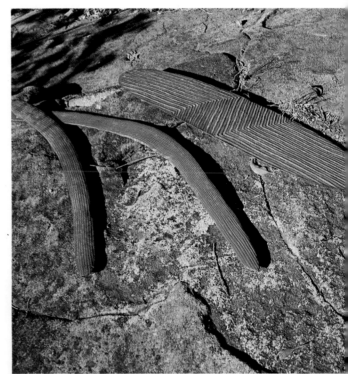

▲ Boomerangs and shield, decorated with carving.

Didgeridu featuring painted designs, Yirrkala. ▶

Doctor's dillybag and the hand of the sorcerer. ▶

▲ Painting on bailer shell, Groote Eylandt.

▼ Lil-lils of western NSW, decorated with intricate incised patterns.

figurative art, that is, by depicting the orifices, in this case of the face—the eyes, nostrils and mouth.

The paintings from Emily Gap featuring a series of vertical lines and three dots (lower picture, page 20) are, according to Basedow, Arunta totemic signs of the witchetty grub group—in local tongue, *Utnguringita*. They were done, say the Arunta, by the Altjerra men (culture heroes) using utnguringita (witchetty grub) fat, but more likely they were done with emu fat as the fluid base for the pigment—this is often used as a fixative and gives permanency. These paintings are very old and are stained into the rock in such a way that they could only be removed by chipping off the surface; rain and normal weathering have little effect on them. Basedow (1925) was told that the designs include the images of women who waited at the foot of the cliff while the men concealed sacred objects in the rocks above, and Mountford (1961) writes that the top sloping line represents a woman looking upwards, the three circles the eggs of a witchetty grub, and the vertical parallel lines the designs which initiated men paint on their bodies when they perform the ceremonies.

Sacred symbolic objects may be temporary or permanent. The *waninga* of central Australia fall into the first group; they are similar in function to nurtunja poles, are constructed with great ritual for a particular ceremony and are destroyed im-

Carved baobab nut, King Sound, WA. ▶

▲ Lindsay Roughsey, Aboriginal artist of Mornington Island.

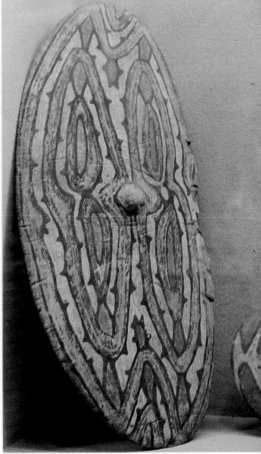

▲ Decorated shield (Baldwin Spencer collection).

Goobalathaldin

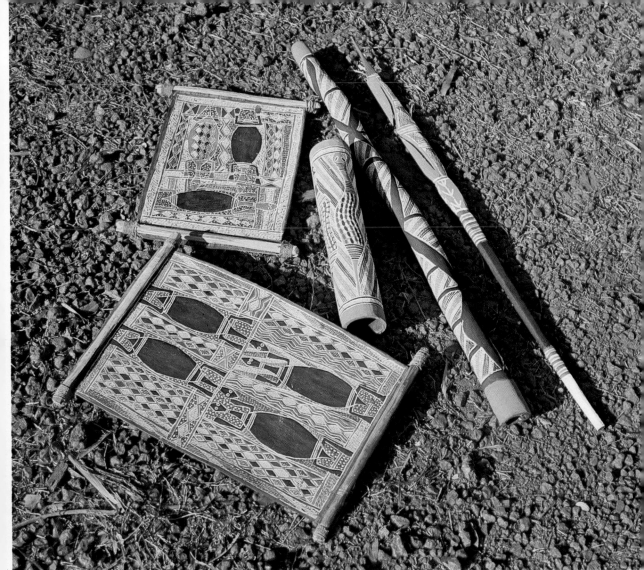

Decorative art of Elcho Island. ▲

mediately afterwards. Waninga are made from human hair, twisted into twine and wound around crossed sticks, then decorated with down, feathers or animal fur. They often feature a rhomboid design and are inhabited for the duration of the ceremony by the totemic creative being. (Basedow links the rhomboid shape to the human form and produces some evidence to support this.) The waninga shown on page 21 is of the Parlltja (snake) totem, Urabunna tribe, and is part of the Baldwin Spencer collection in the National Museum, Melbourne. Permanent sacred objects include *tjuringa*, small engraved stones which are carried on the person, and carved wooden boards which are stored in cave sanctuaries protected by sacred paintings. Both feature similar patterns of circles within circles, loops within loops, sets of parallel, straight and curved lines. These objects enbody the totemic ancestors and the incised designs illustrate in symbolic form one or another of the stories of creation.

'Art for art's sake' is a concept foreign to Aboriginal culture. Their languages have no words which correspond exactly with 'art' and 'artist' though there are terms for the different

Bark painting, Arnhem Land. ▶

▲ Old man of Elcho paints while companion plays didgeridu.

techniques of painting, carving and incising. Art, it seems, is a subsidiary element in the whole of life, with no need for a special name. It is used with great purpose in ceremonial rituals and magic, in teaching and the telling of tales. Perhaps it is in the decoration of utilitarian objects that the Aboriginal comes closest to the Western concept—of art to give pleasure, art to give expression to the creative urge of the individual artist. Implements such as boomerangs, spears, dillybags and didgeridus are rarely sacred and rarely undecorated. Sometimes they are ceremonial—spears, for example, which couldn't possibly be used for actual hunting—but these are not regarded with any special reverence and, generally speaking, the decorated implements are completely functional and already perfectly formed for their particular purpose before the maker spent hour after hour adorning them, apparently purely to satisfy his aesthetic impulses. In eastern Australia almost everything used was elaborately decorated, in southern areas mostly by engraving, possibly because the hardwoods used lost no strength when carved. Lil lils, bladed clubs confined to New South Wales and certain areas of southern Queensland, are particularly noticeable artistically for the tremendous control of carved line, extremely difficult to obtain on hard timber. Further north there was a greater tendency to painted decorations, manifested first by red ochre rubbed into the grooves, then by a combination of painting and carving, then by painting alone. Skin rugs, common in colder parts, had abstract patterns scratched on the inner surface of the hides. Utensils such as wooden carrying dishes were decorated with intricate engraved patterns and even the large grinding stones of the women often had designs carved on the under-surface, though these could not be seen unless the heavy mortar was overturned. Rarely are stories of any totemic import carved on implements, utensils and weapons, but rather designs which are easily recognisable as symbolised forms of animal tracks, yams, and so on. Thus a series of lozenge-shaped objects on a boomerang or spear may represent a kangaroo running, and the marks alongside may be the tracks of the hunter. Mountford maintains that these painted and incised patterns on

▲ Carved figure from Groote Eylandt is totemic in character.

▼ Wadamu, artist of Elcho, with some of his work.

painting, north-eastern Arnhem Land. ▼Bark painting, Elcho Island   ▲ Bark painting collected by Sir W. Baldwin Spencer.

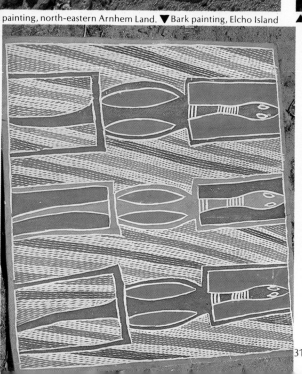

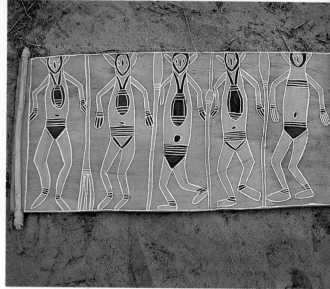

▲ Contemporary painting tells story of the doctors. Artist: Wadamu.

▼ Painting by Wadamu, Elcho Island.

▲ Artist and his work, Umbakumba, Groote Eylandt.

mundane objects are the personal marks of the maker, serving a similar purpose to the coat-of-arms on the shield of a mediaeval knight, and Elkin suggests that they may be linked with economic needs, magical puri-puris making the weapon not just more pleasing but more powerful. However, richly grained timbers were not usually further embellished but simply stained with vegetable juices and beautifully polished, lending weight to a theory of art for its own sake.

Dillybags and carrying baskets made of twine or bark were invariably colourfully decorated, particularly in northern areas where the bark baskets often feature different designs on each side. Baskets are used by both men and women, the latter for food-gathering and the former for carrying sacred objects. Illustrated (page 26) is a doctor's bag which probably contains the tools of his sorcery. The powerful thumbnail of the holder is doubtless used for sacred art; in many forms it is not permitted to use anything other than the human body, so that a thumbnail long enough and strong enough for carving is essential. Carving on baobab nuts is a form of Aboriginal decorative art confined to the King Sound area of north-western Australia (page 26).

It seems that the practice of painting on bark was widespread

◀ Bark painting, Arnhem Land.

▲ It is cured over a flame, outer side down . . .

then trodden flat and buried in sand to season. ▲

▼ Wadamu and his son remove bark from selected stringy-bark tree.

throughout Australia and Tasmania wherever suitable materials were available, but few examples of this art have survived from southern Australia and none from Tasmania. This was because early colonists paid little attention to Aboriginal culture and by the time interest was aroused, bark painting was a lost art in the more settled areas. Early collectors were few, but the works they preserved are some of the best examples of Aboriginal art in existence—probably only because they had a greater range to choose from than is now available. It must be remembered that the major part of the art of the Aboriginal people of Australia was intended to last only for a short time; the bark paintings we see in museums might be fifty or even a hundred years old, but in Aboriginal society they would have lasted at most but a few years, and in many cases would have been ceremonially destroyed almost immediately after creation. Today the only people still painting on bark are the tribes of the tropical north, of Arnhem Land, the Gulf of Carpentaria, and adjacent off-shore islands. Here, bark painting, always a vital art form, is flourishing and playing an increasingly important role.

In these tropical regions, where bark wet season shelters are the tradition, bark paintings reached the highest stage of development. Aboriginals have more time on their hands in the wet season, and many anthropologists hold that the art of

Aboriginal art is a family affair—artist's 'studio', Yirrkala. ▶

33

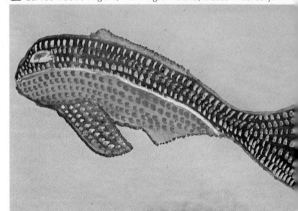

Carved wooden figure, Mornington Island, is used in sorcery. ▲

bark painting originated in the casual decoration of seasonal shelters to while away the rainy days. Traditionally, art styles and techniques vary from one region to another, influenced by factors such as isolation and the availability of materials. On Groote Eylandt there are no deposits of red ochre, and this material must be obtained by trade from the adjacent mainland; but Groote is an island of manganese ore, source of black pigment, and here the traditional style consists of single or grouped figures on a plain black background. At Mornington Island, on the opposite side of the Gulf of Carpentaria, the reverse is the case—black figures are against a white background. On Melville Island, off Arnhem Land to the west, there are plentiful supplies of red, white and yellow ochres, and these colours predominate over black, which is obtainable only in the form of powdered charcoal. The art tradition there is abstract, consisting of highly formalised, non-figurative designs bearing little relation to that of the nearby mainland from which it is effectively isolated by the treacherous tidal straits of Dundas and Clarence. Western Arnhem Land is the home of the intriguing x-ray paintings, stylised but essentially realistic art in which the internal features as well as the external appearance of the subject are depicted. X-ray barks seldom consist of more than one or at the most two figures, usually painted on a background of plain red. Another distinctive art style in western Arnhem Land bark paintings depicts the stick-like, animated Mimi spirit people, an adaptation of an ancient cave art the present-day Aboriginals disown. Barks from north-eastern Arnhem Land, however, differ remarkably from those of all other areas; the art style is more colourful and more complex, made up from a wide range of abstract and naturalistic motifs. The crowded, detailed paintings are directly linked with religion, and destruction of sacred sites at Yirrkala (Gove) threatens one of the most productive areas of Aboriginal art in Australia, for without his land the Aboriginal has no heart to paint.

Shapes of the Rainbow Serpent; watercolours by Dick Roughsey. ◆

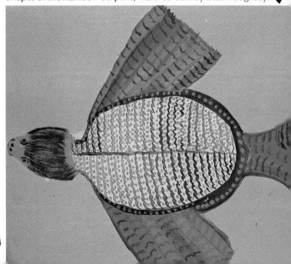